THE LITTLE INSTRUCTION BOOK FOR

Cat Parents

a Hilarious
survival
Guide for
cat owners

ILLUSTRATED BY
FIN KENDALL

KATE FREEMAN

summersdale

THE LITTLE INSTRUCTION BOOK FOR CAT PARENTS

Copyright © Octopus Publishing Group Limited, 2024

Text by Lucy York
Illustrations by Fin Kendall

An Hachette UK Company
www.hachette.co.uk

Summersdale Publishers
Part of Octopus Publishing Group Limited
Carmelite House
50 Victoria Embankment
LONDON
EC4Y 0DZ
UK

www.summersdale.com

The authorized representative in the EEA is Hachette Ireland, 8 Castlecourt Centre, Castleknock Road, Castleknock, Dublin 15, D15 YF6A, Ireland.

Printed and bound in Poland

ISBN: 978-1-83799-362-8

This FSC® label means that materials used for the product have been responsibly sourced

MIX
Paper | Supporting responsible forestry
FSC® C018236

Substantial discounts on bulk quantities of Summersdale books are available to corporations, professional associations and other organizations. For details contact general enquiries: telephone: +44 (0) 1243 771107 or email: enquiries@summersdale.com.

Introduction

Congratulations, you're a cat parent! Or should that be cat butler?

While your cat may rule your household with an iron paw, it is a very cute paw. With little toe beans. It is a pleasure to serve under these elegant creatures who, let us not forget, were once worshipped as gods.

Whether you're a newbie or an old hand at the role, this no-nonsense handbook will guide you through the warm, purry and sometimes stormy waters of sharing your home with a feline.

After all, being a cat parent is not a choice, but a lifestyle!

Dietary requirements
may change at any time.
Consider carefully before
bulk-ordering.

It is essential to
keep your cat's bowl
topped up with fresh
water at all times.

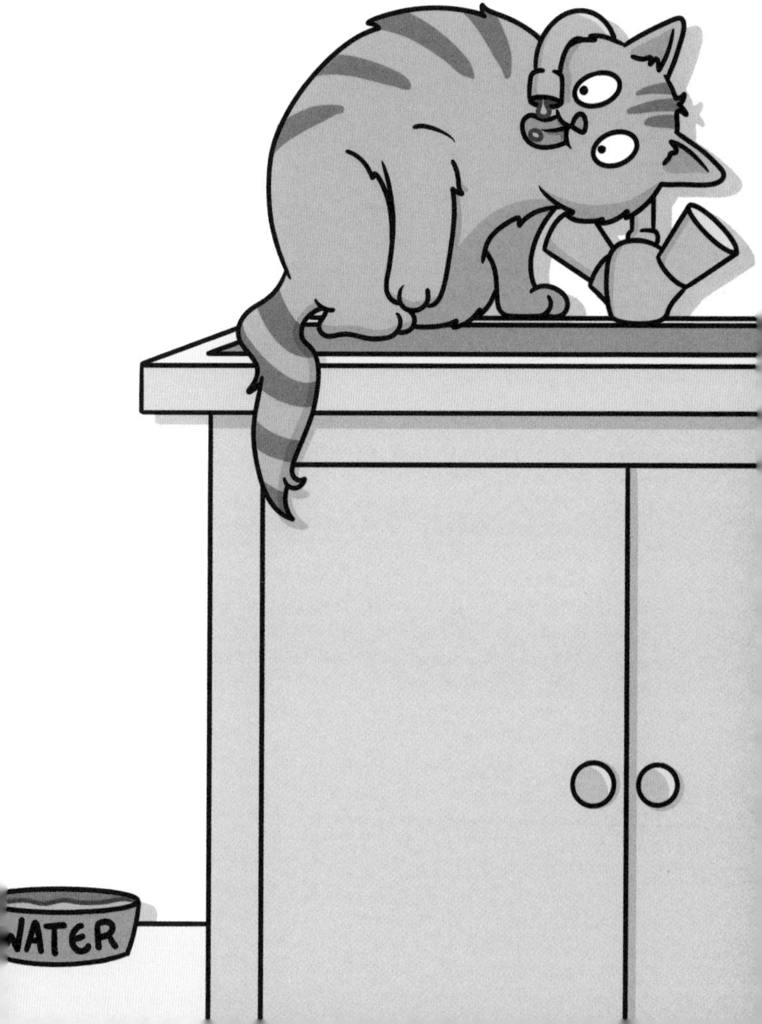
WATER

Working hours will be
strictly regulated by your
furry supervisor.

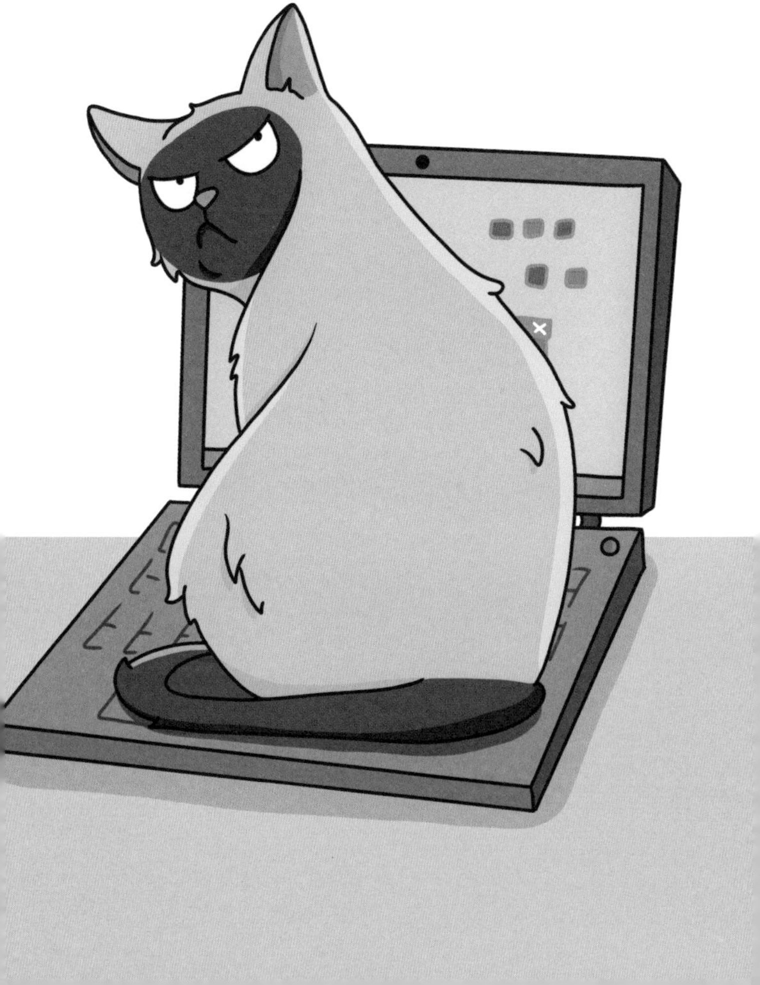

When your cat brings
you gifts, it is customary
to express gratitude.

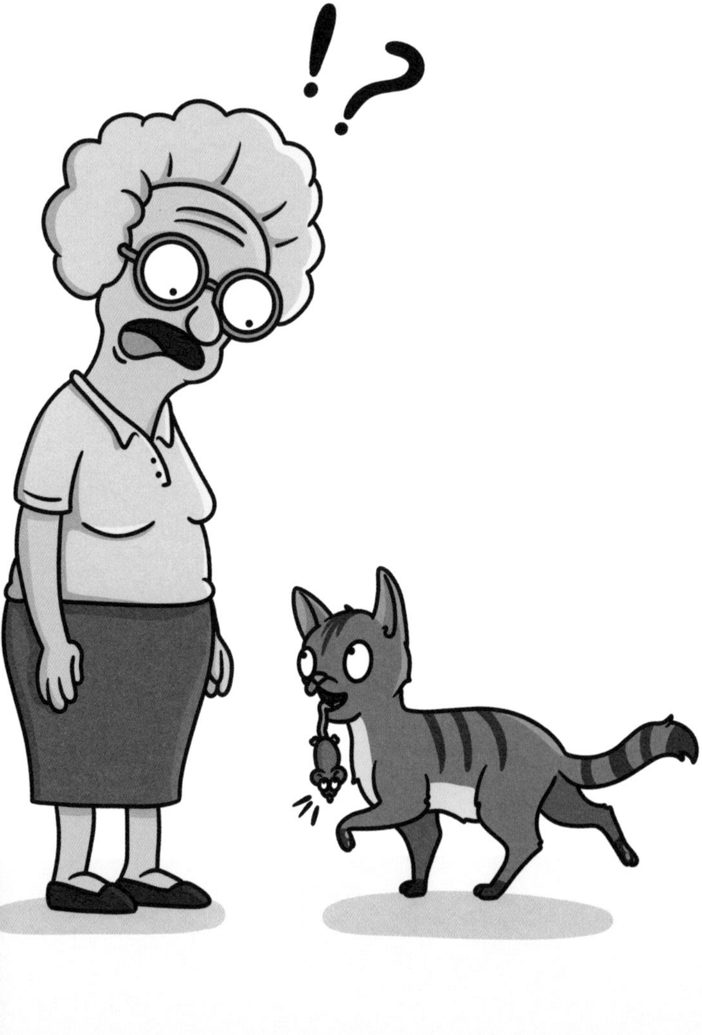
!?

Unauthorized absences
by human staff will be
dealt with accordingly.

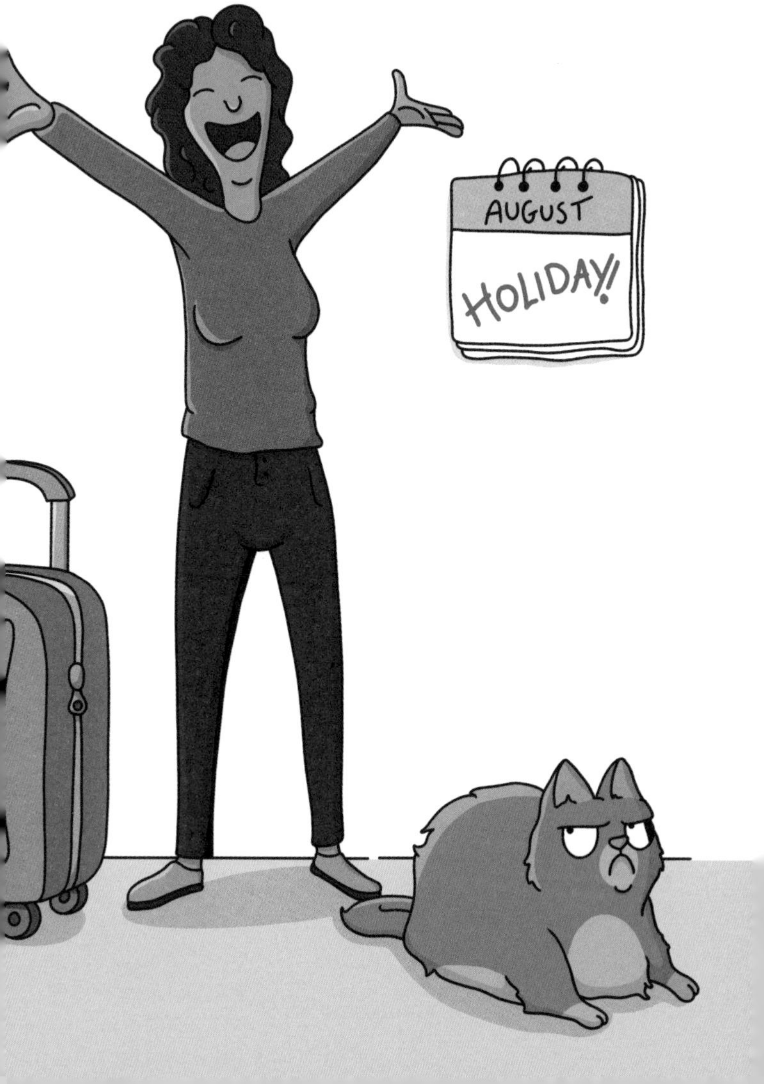
AUGUST
HOLIDAY!

Your cat will ensure
that surfaces are kept
clear and tidy.

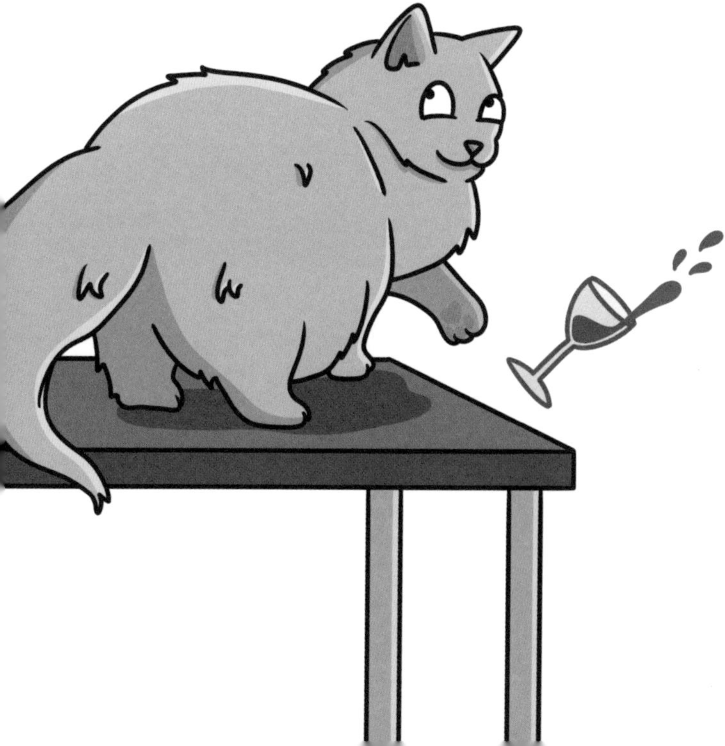

The cat flap is merely a suggestion. Be ready to get up and open the door whenever required.

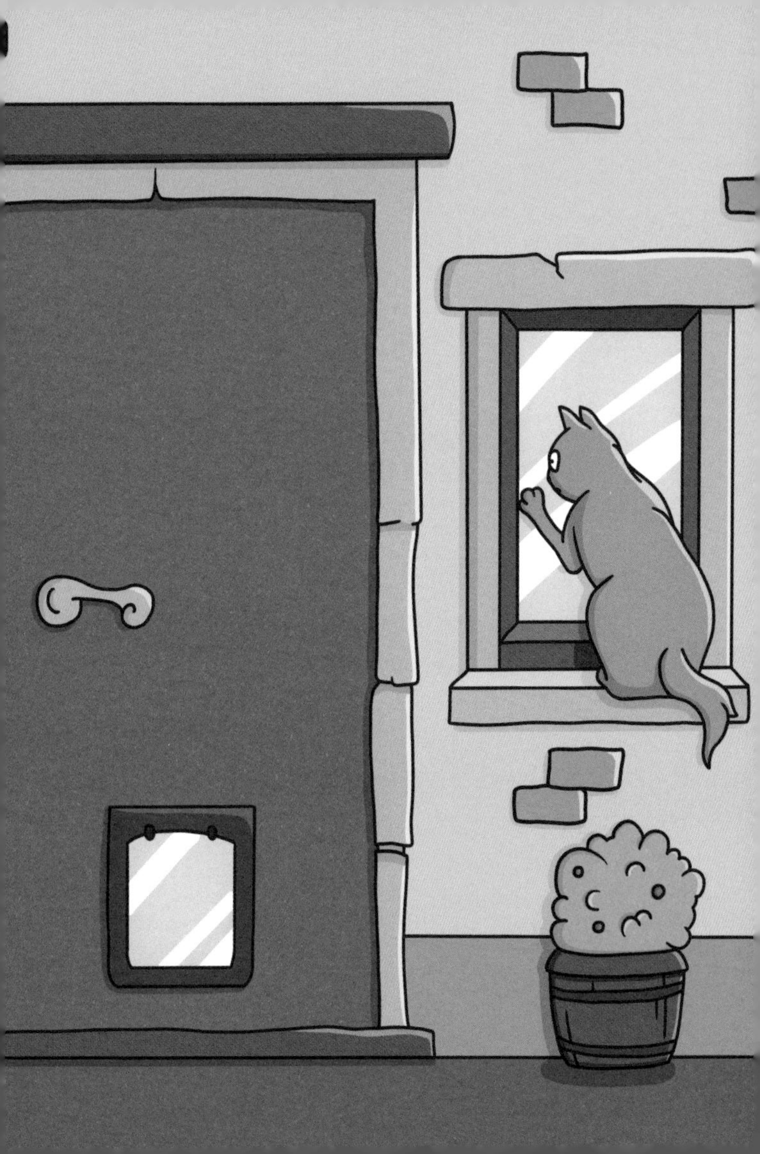

Cats are playful creatures. One game they particularly love is leaving "treasures" hidden around the house for you to find.

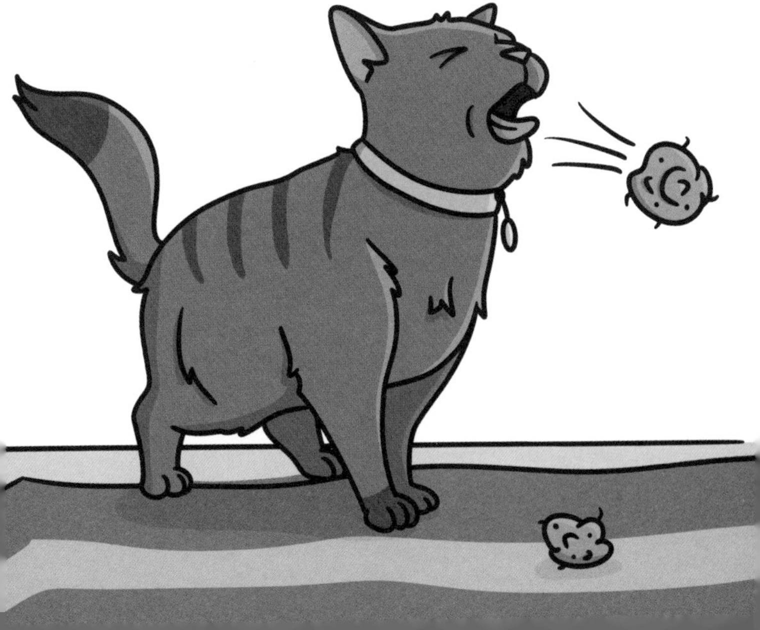

Cats make perfect
bed companions.

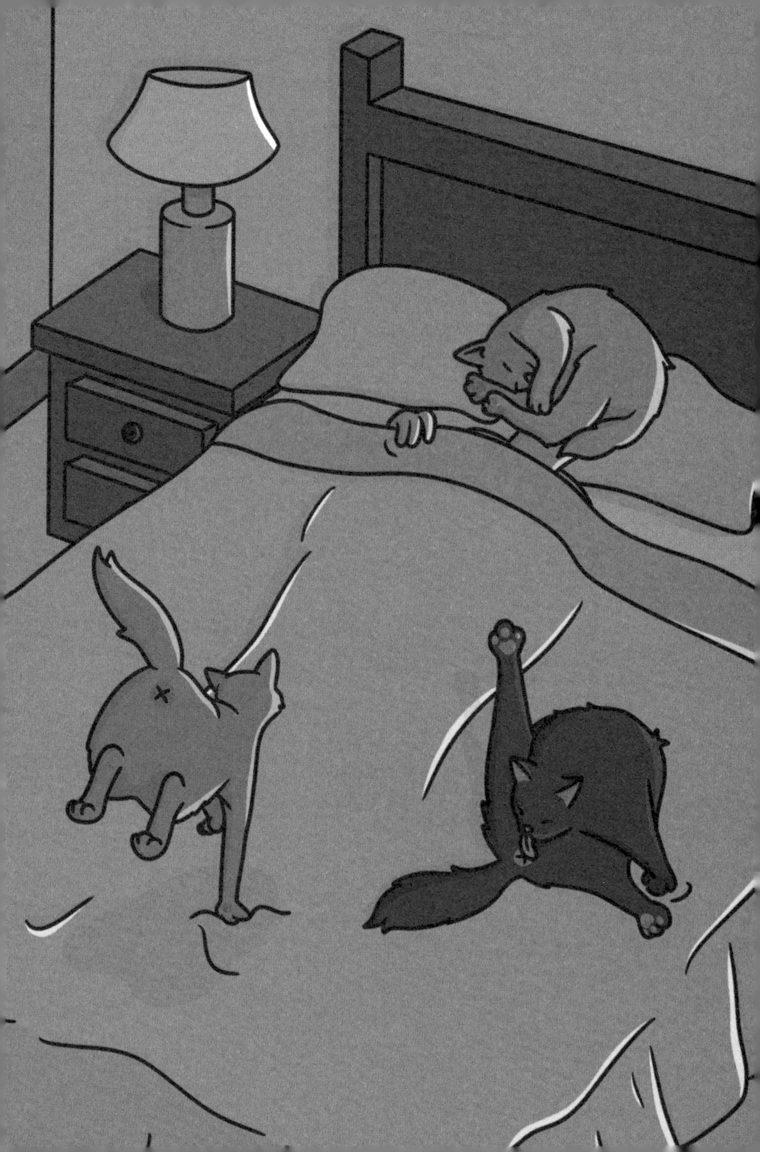

A good scratching
post is an essential piece
of kit that every cat
parent should invest in.

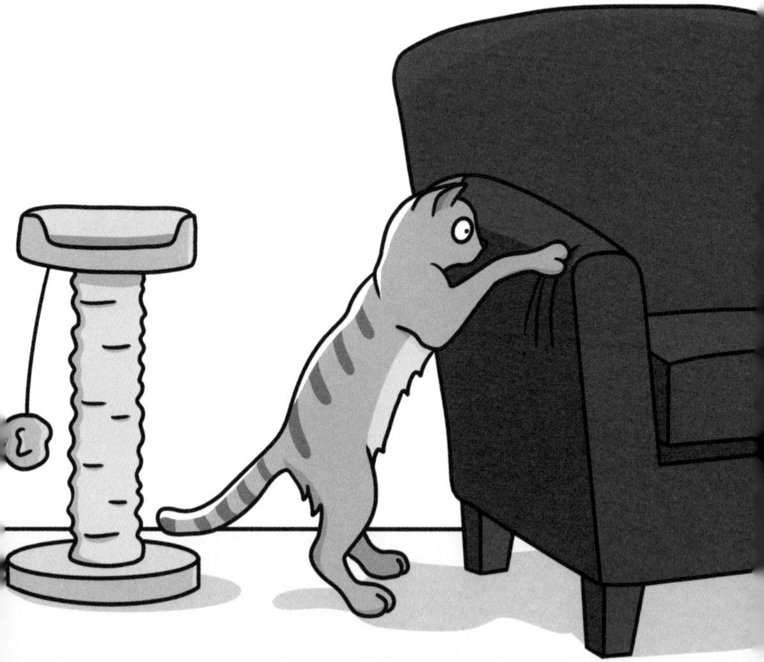

As a cat parent you can bin your alarm clock. You won't be needing that again.

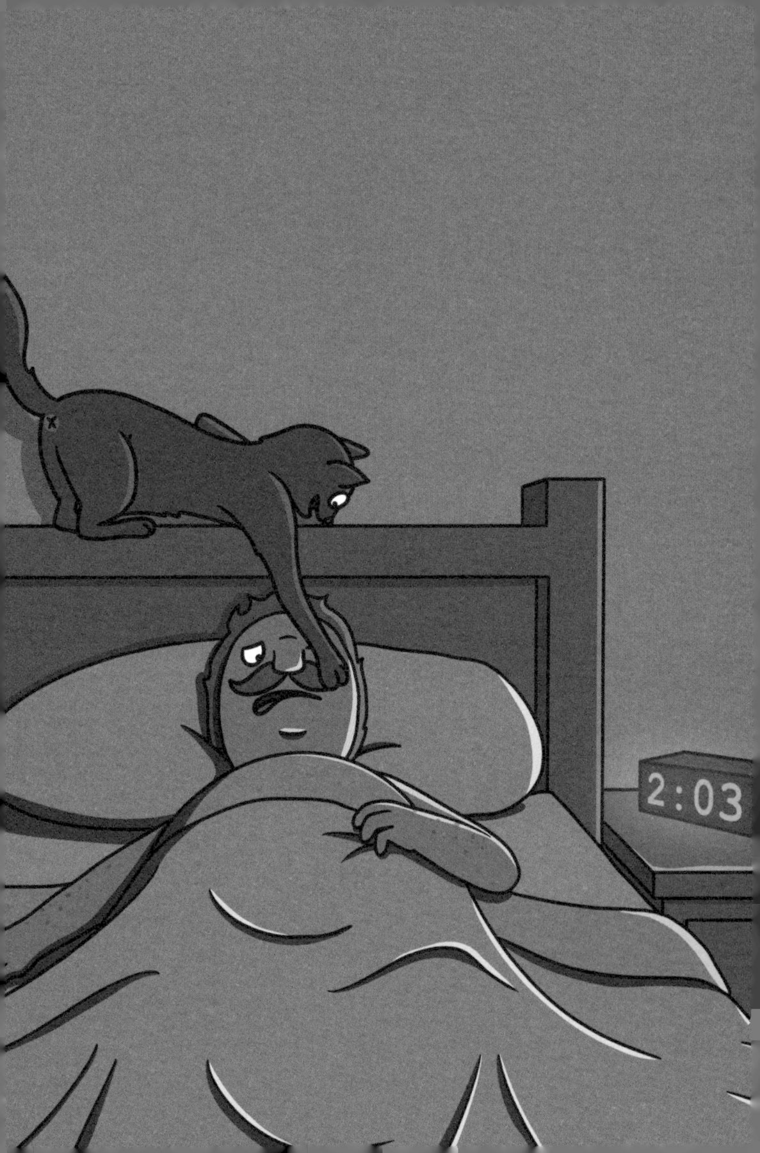
2:03

All new items brought
into the home must be
inspected immediately.

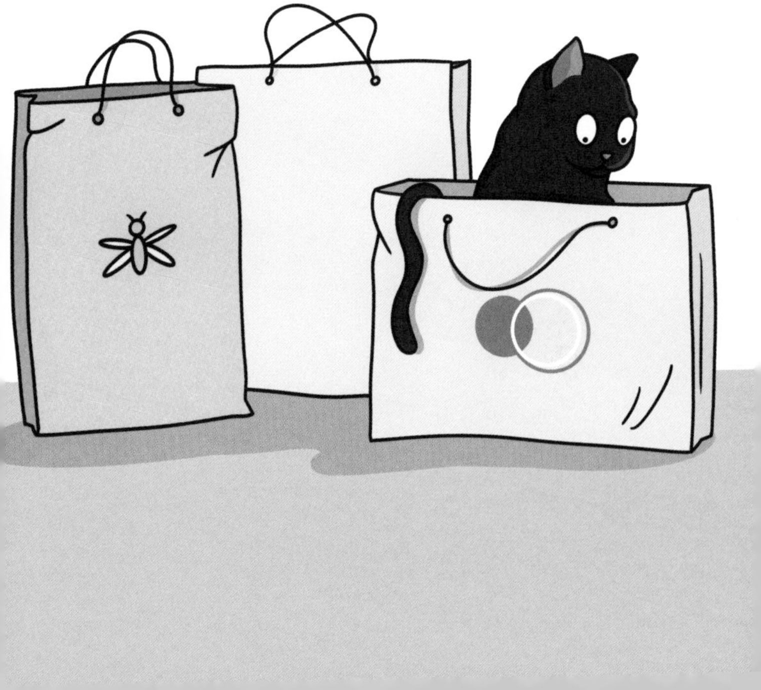

They may not always
show it, but your cat
appreciates all the drinks
you make for them.

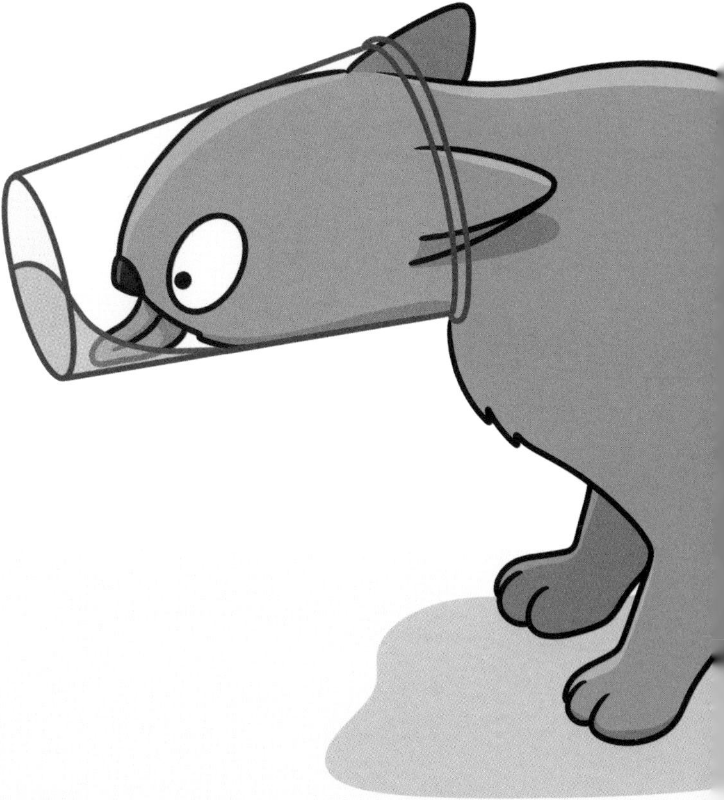

Cats love Christmas
— but don't be surprised
if they demonstrate
exacting standards when
it comes to decorating.

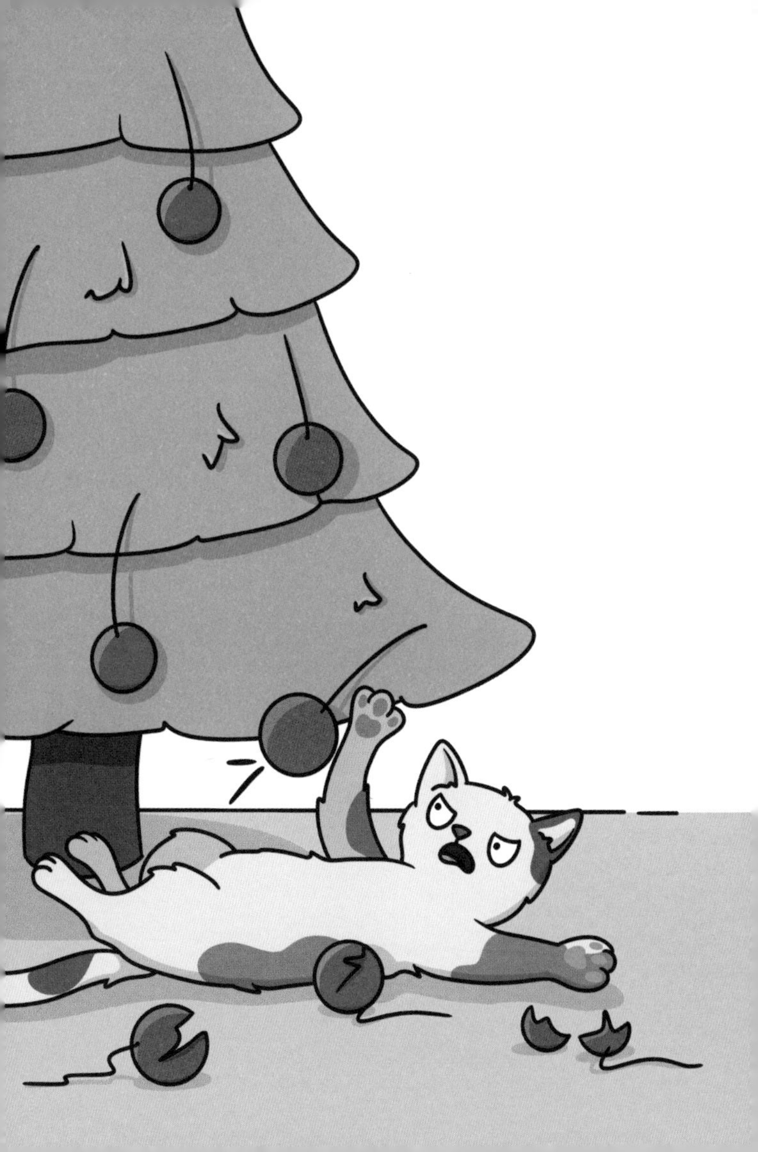

Your cat will protect you from any threat that may be lurking beneath a blanket.

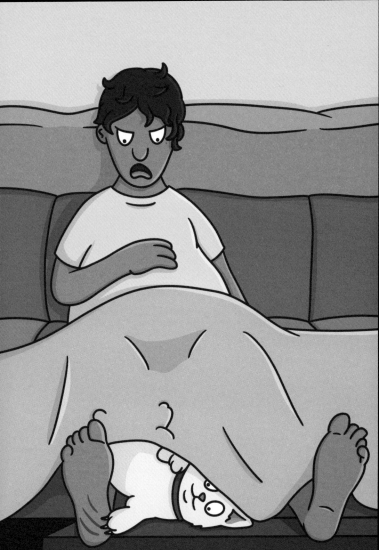

You won't be needing a
personal trainer any more.
Your cat will keep you
on your toes.

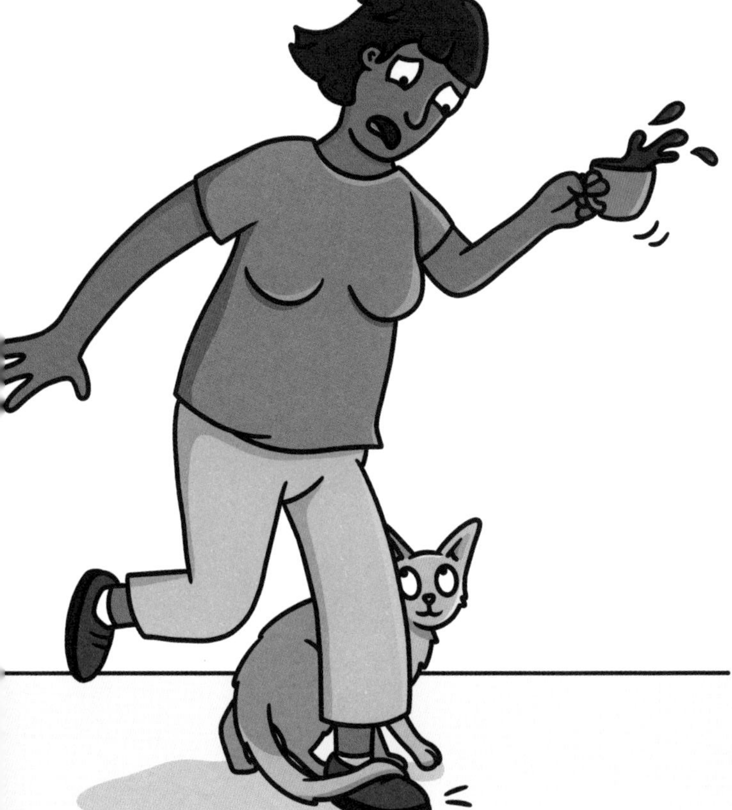

It is standard practice for cat parents to erect a shrine to their beloved kitty.

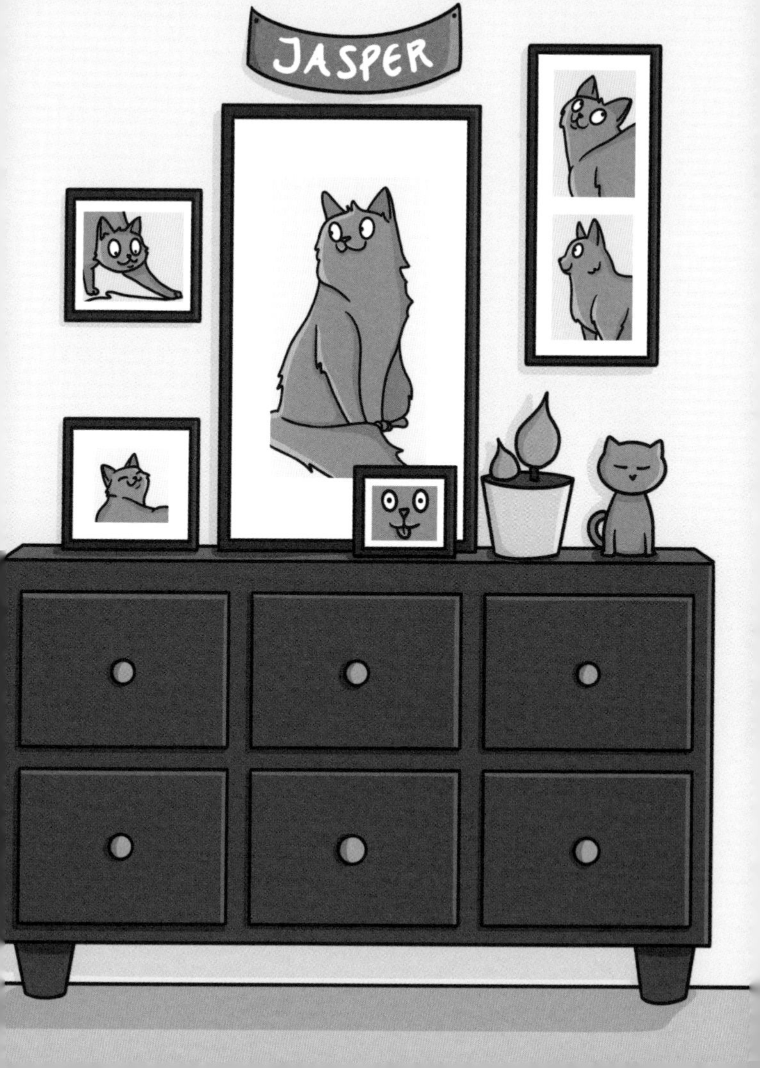
JASPER

Your cat knows that
sharing is caring.

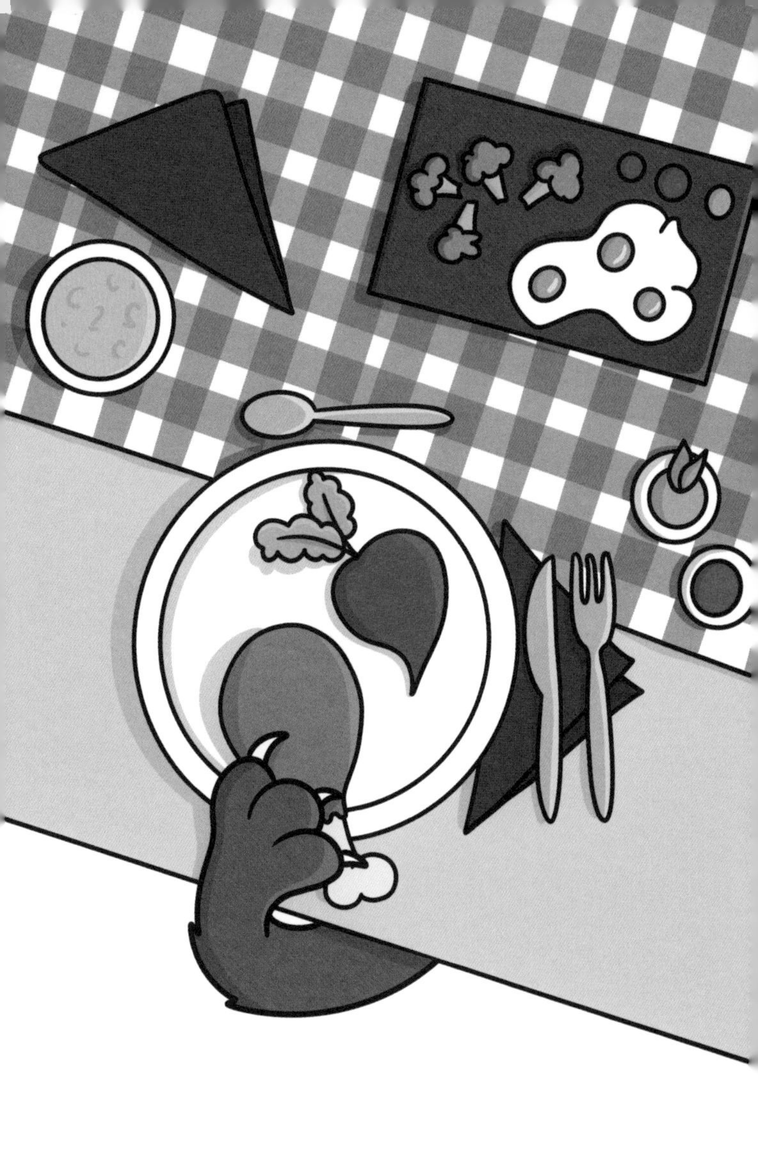

A cat's belly may be rubbed only a specific number of times before the attack sequence is initiated. Good luck figuring out how many times that is.

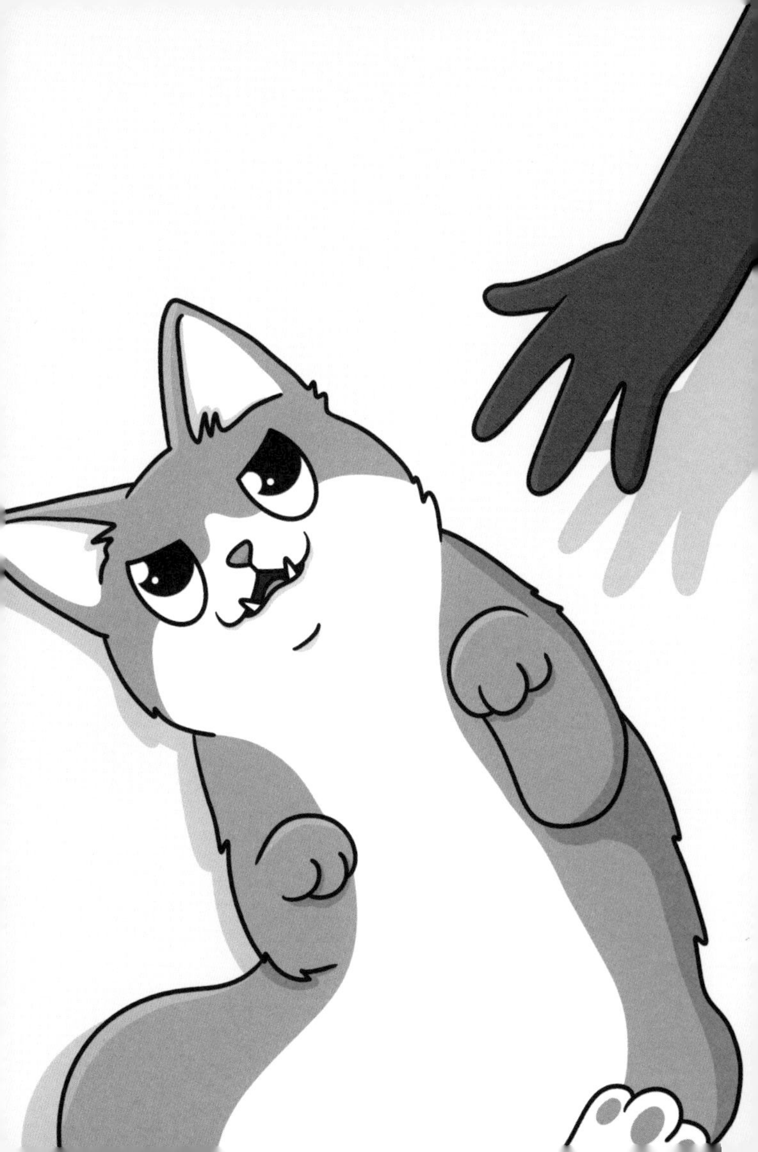

Whatever you are
doing, it is always less
important than giving
your cat attention.

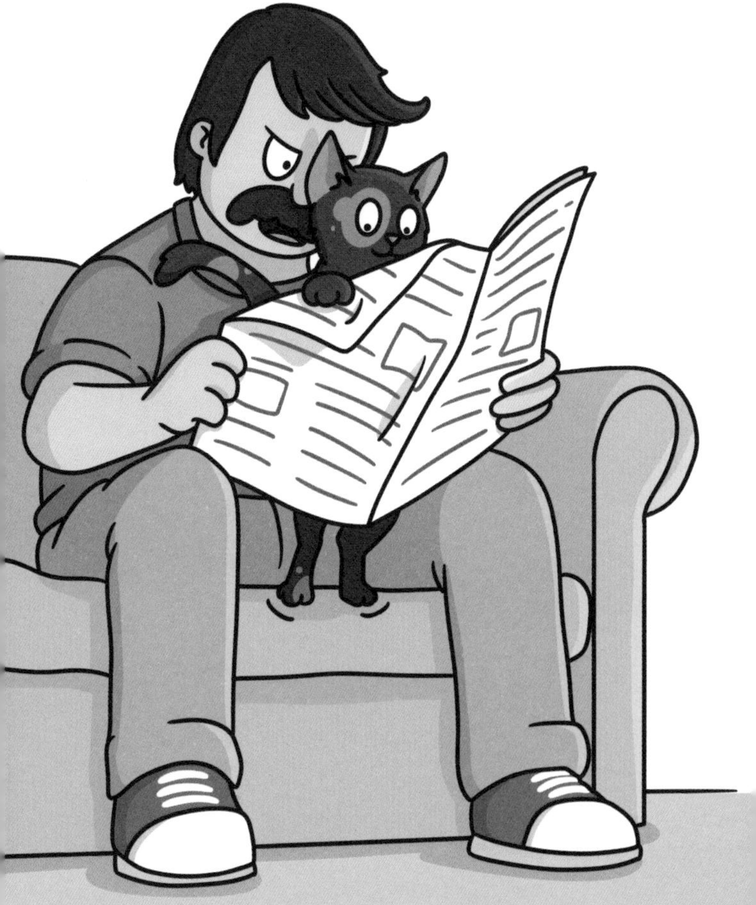

One of the important roles your cat plays in your home is toilet chaperone. Be sure to leave the bathroom door open at all times to facilitate this.

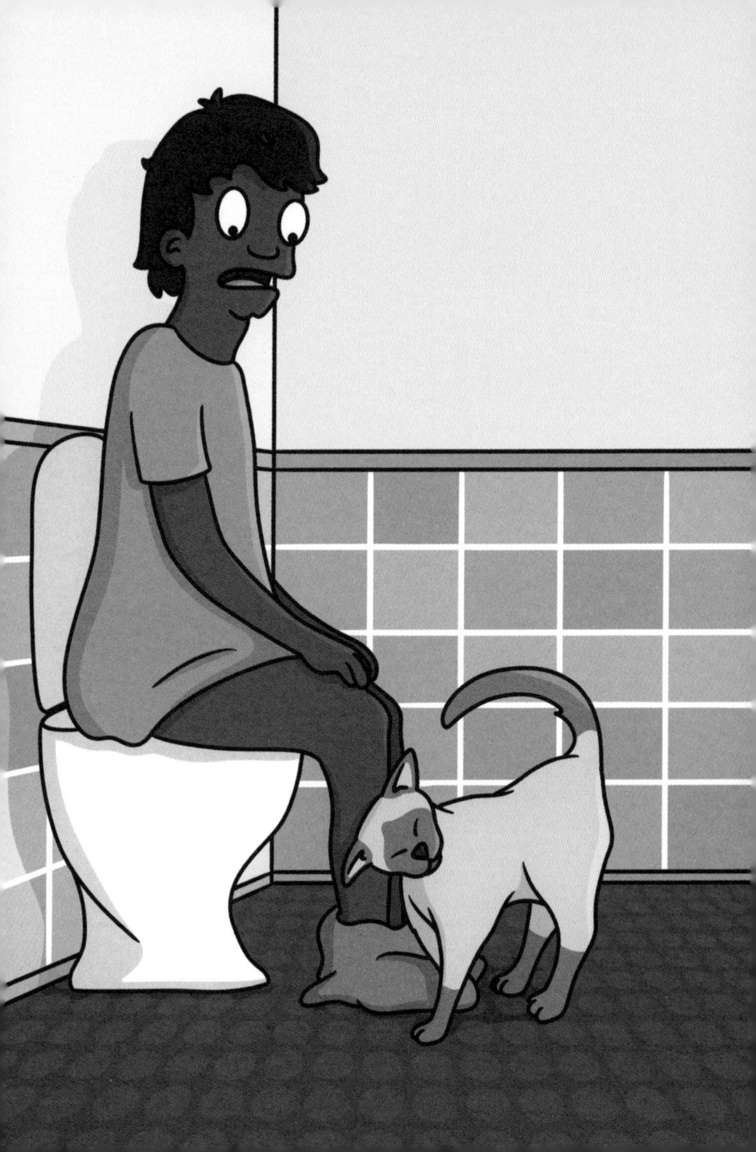

Some boxes are safe
for your cat to enter.
Some are not.

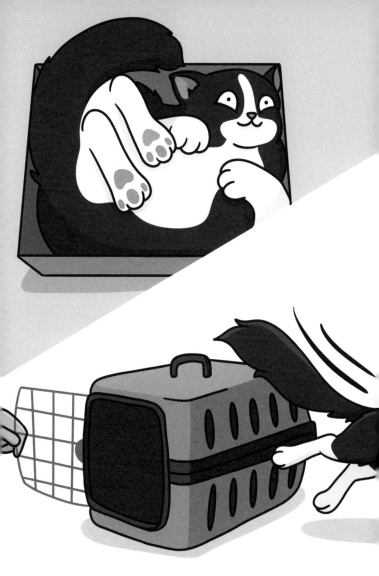

If you listen carefully at about 3 a.m., you may be lucky enough to hear your cat singing the song of their people.

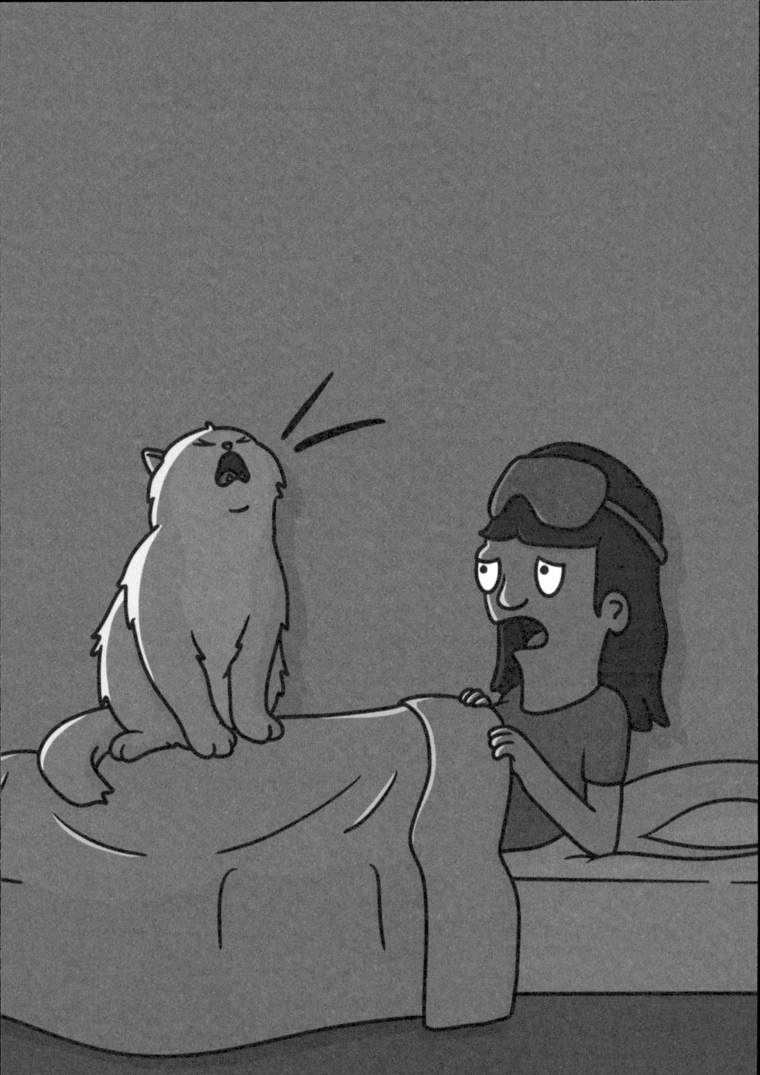

Should you need to summon your cat, you need only sound the international feline emergency call, which can be reproduced by shaking a bag of treats.

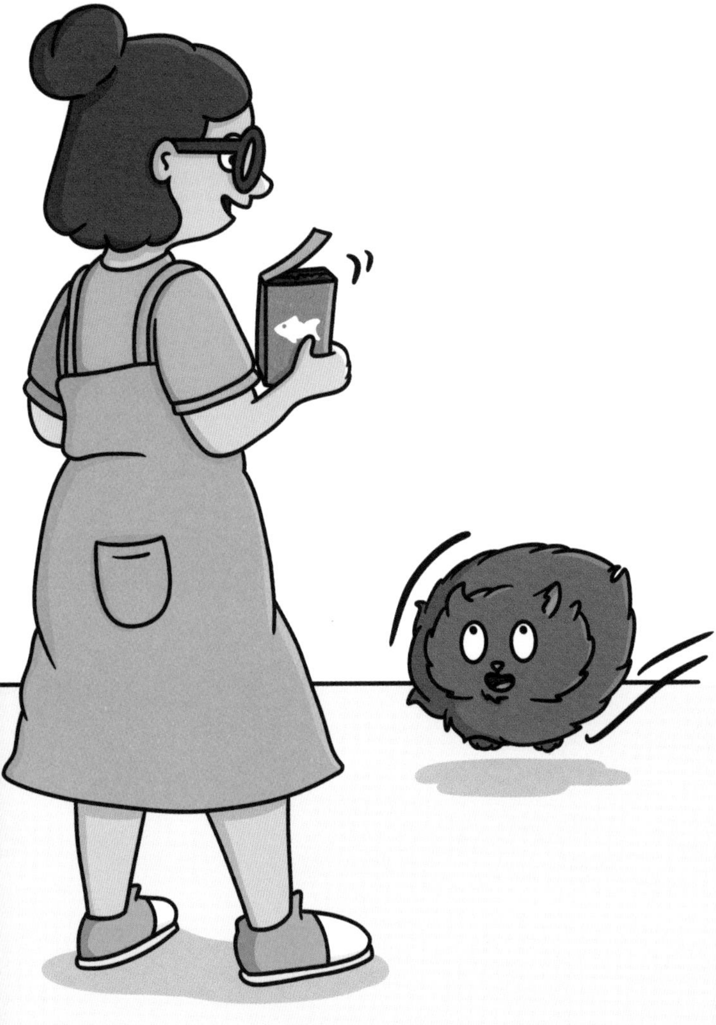

Once you become
a cat parent, you will
never stretch alone.

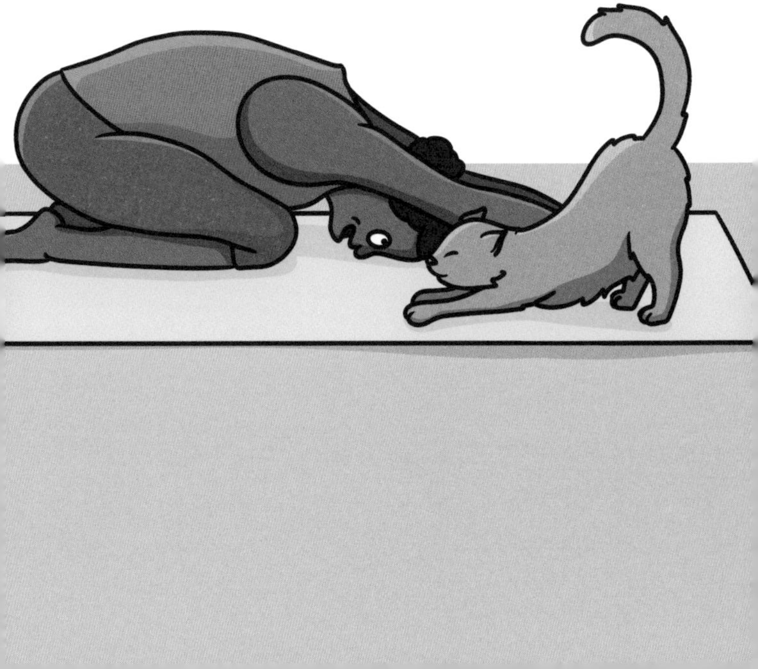

You can count on
your cat to arrive
right on time for
important meetings.

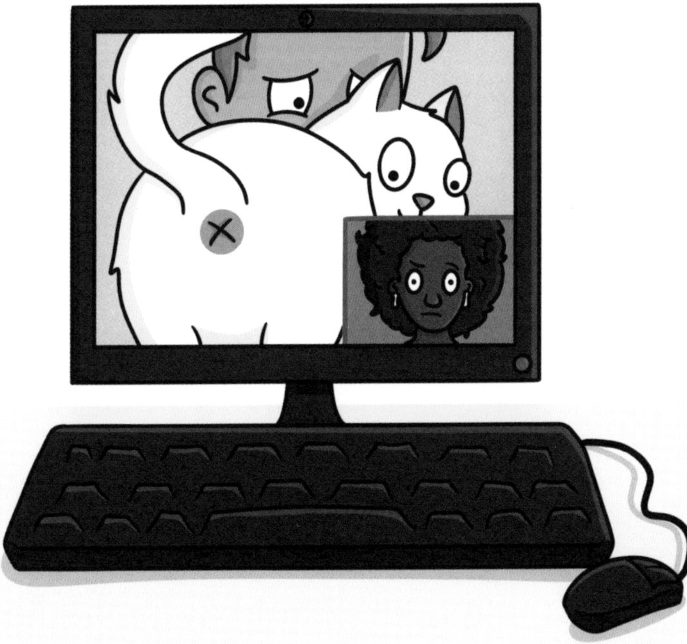

Litter trays are a great option for your cat's toileting needs. With emphasis on the word "option".

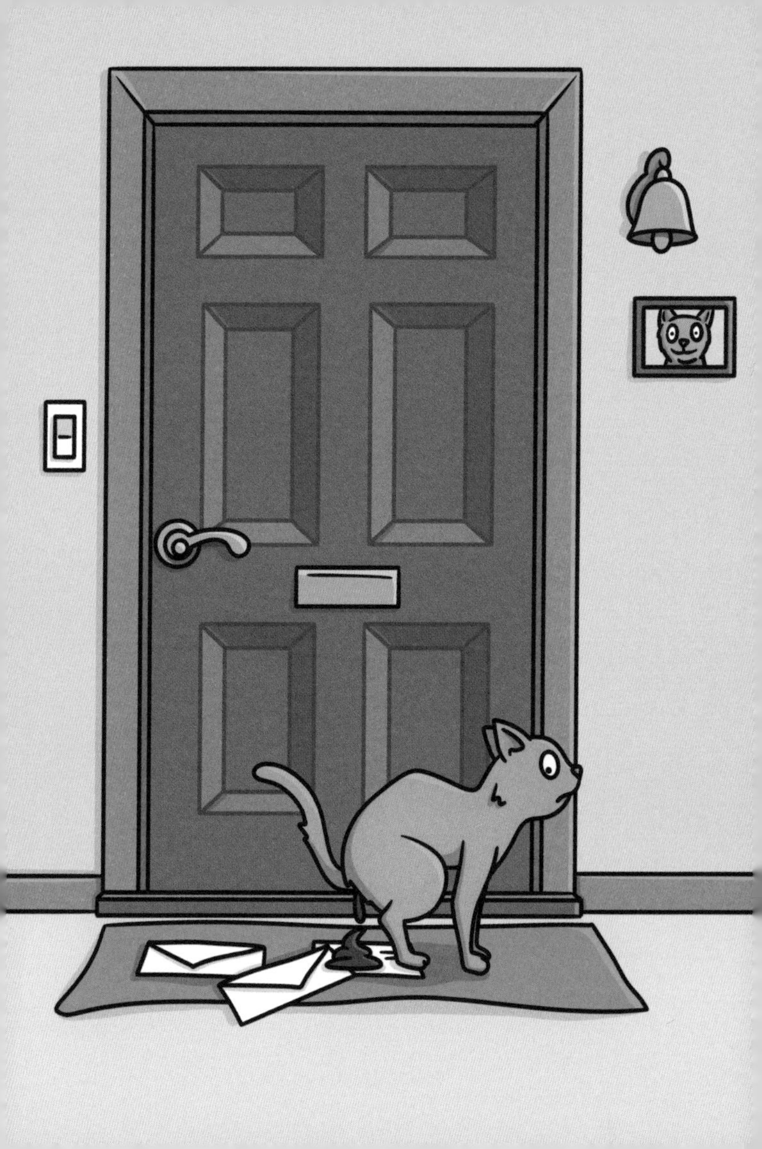

When it comes to removing cat hair, the vacuum cleaner is your friend — but remember that it is your cat's sworn enemy.

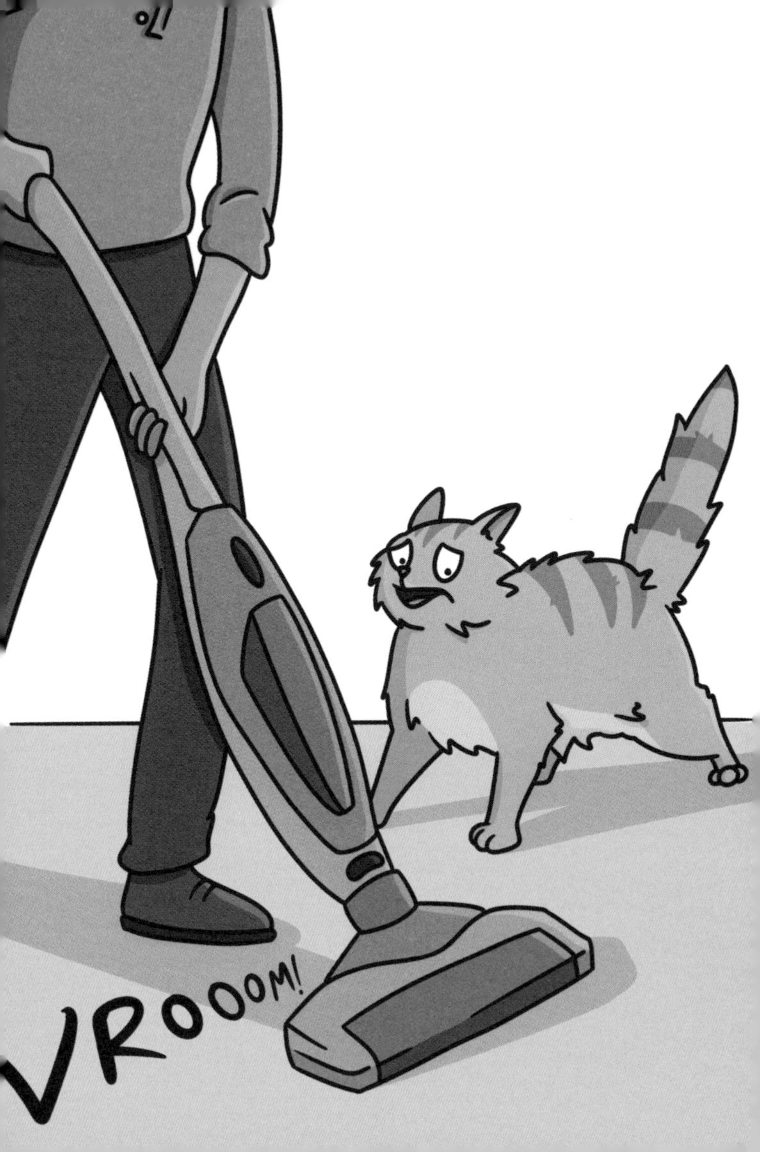
VROOOM!

Your cat is a natural artist. Appreciate their work, should they deign to create any for you.

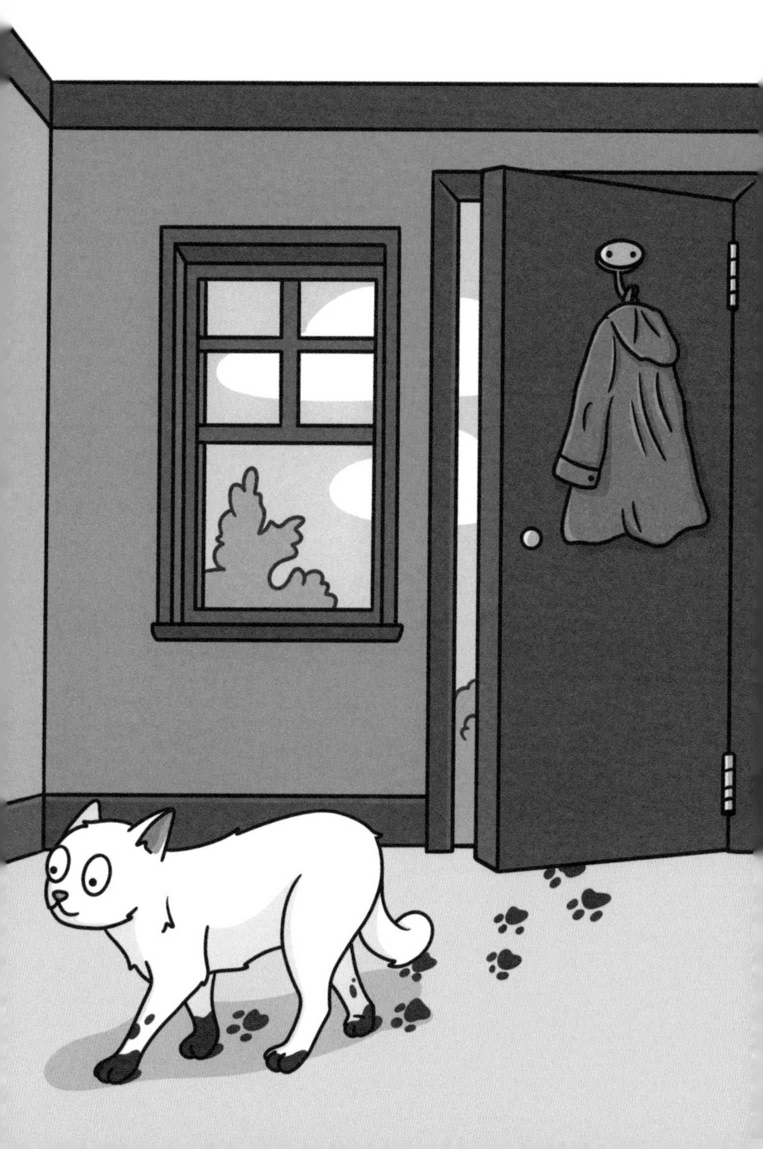

Your cat may commence
a deep tissue massage at
precisely the moment when
you want to get up to use
the toilet. If this happens,
the correct procedure is
to remain perfectly still.

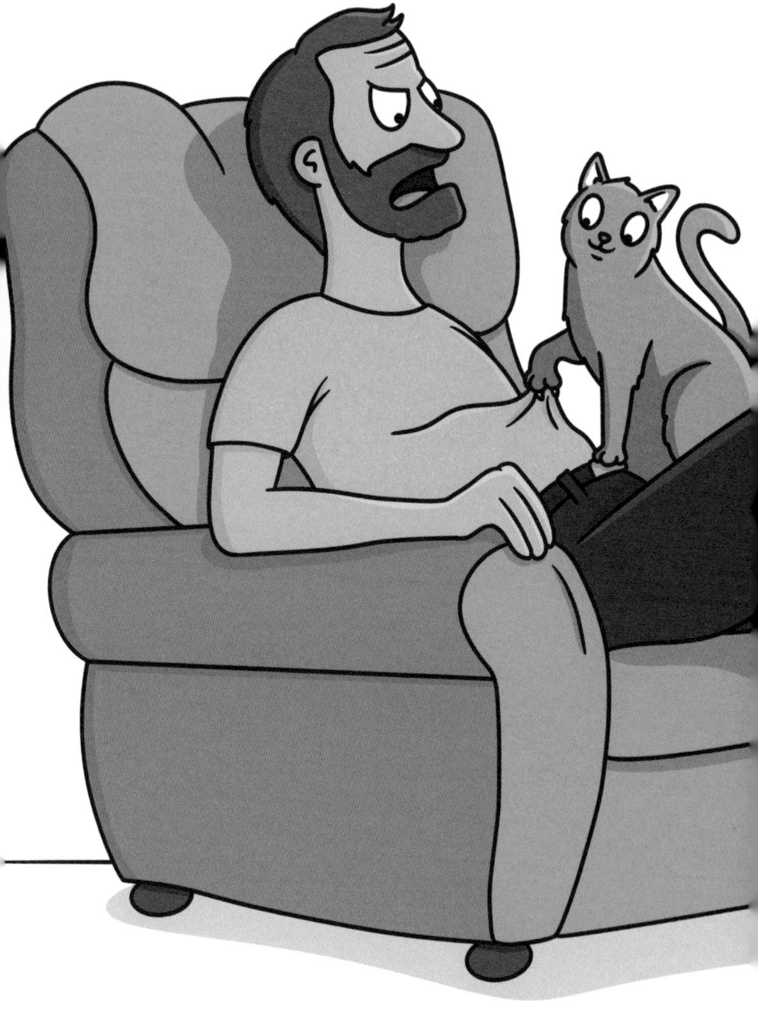

Seating preferences will be clearly indicated and should not be challenged.

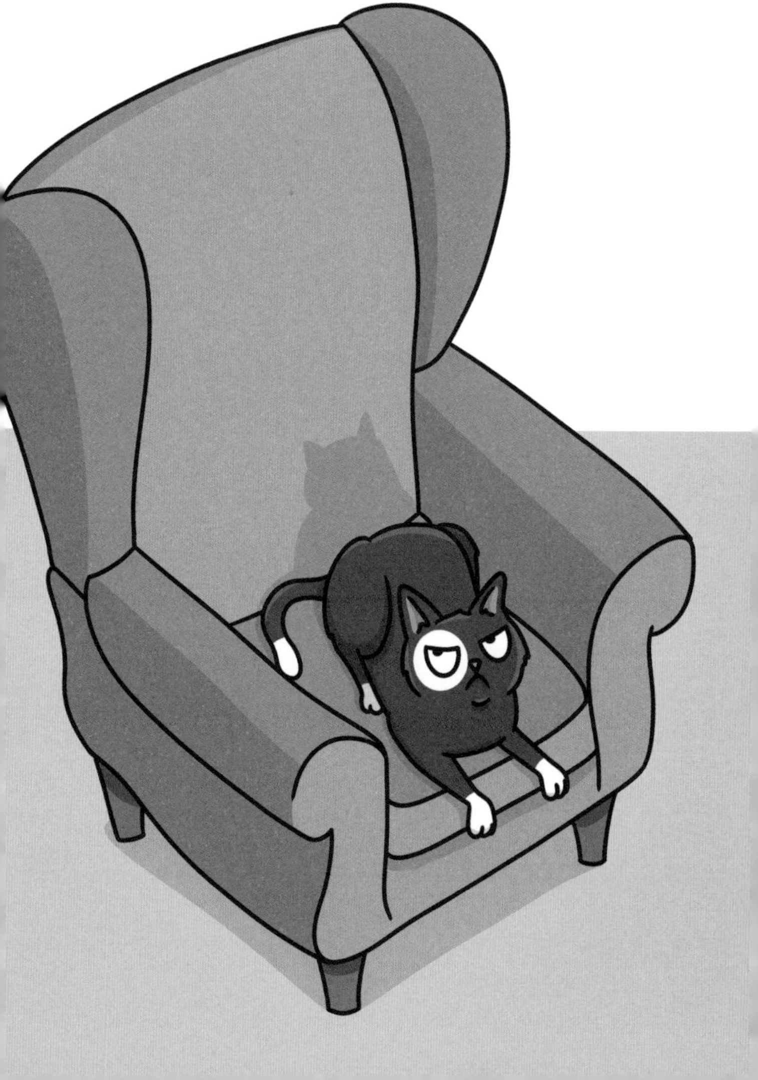

Though there is no
known instance in recorded
history of a feline actually
catching The Little Red Dot
That Moves, your cat will
valiantly try to do so.

If you can't find
your cat, don't panic.
They will always be in the
last place you look.

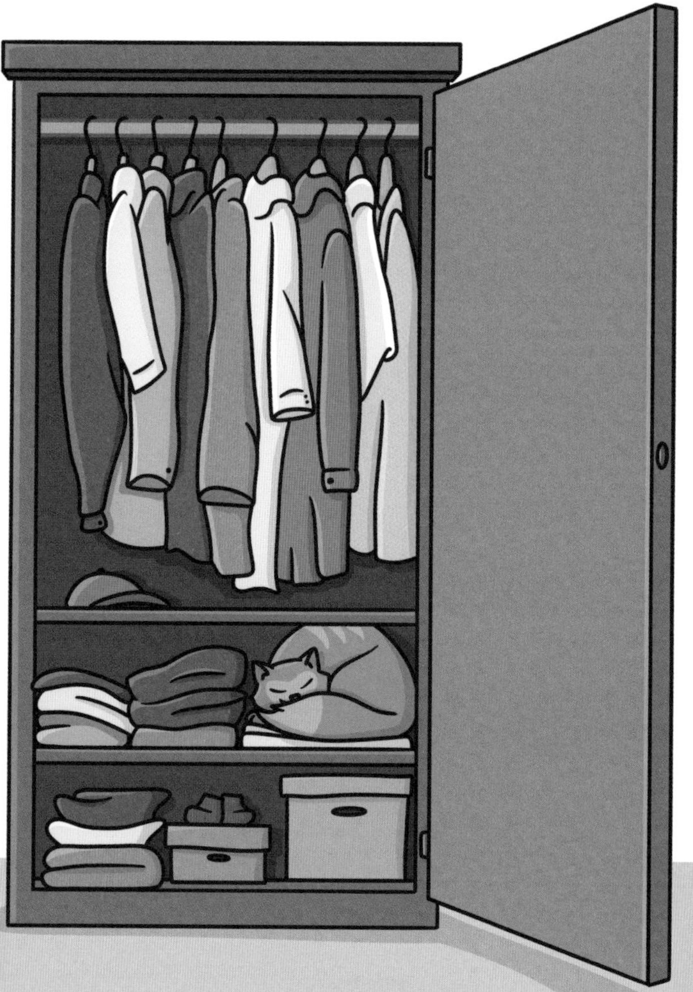

There is nothing
more interesting than
watching your cat.

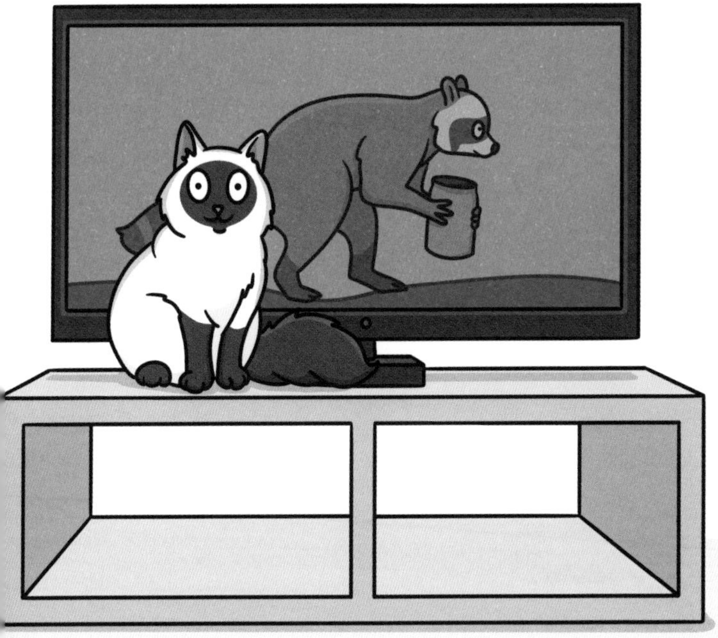

Your cat will
alert you to any
invisible threats.

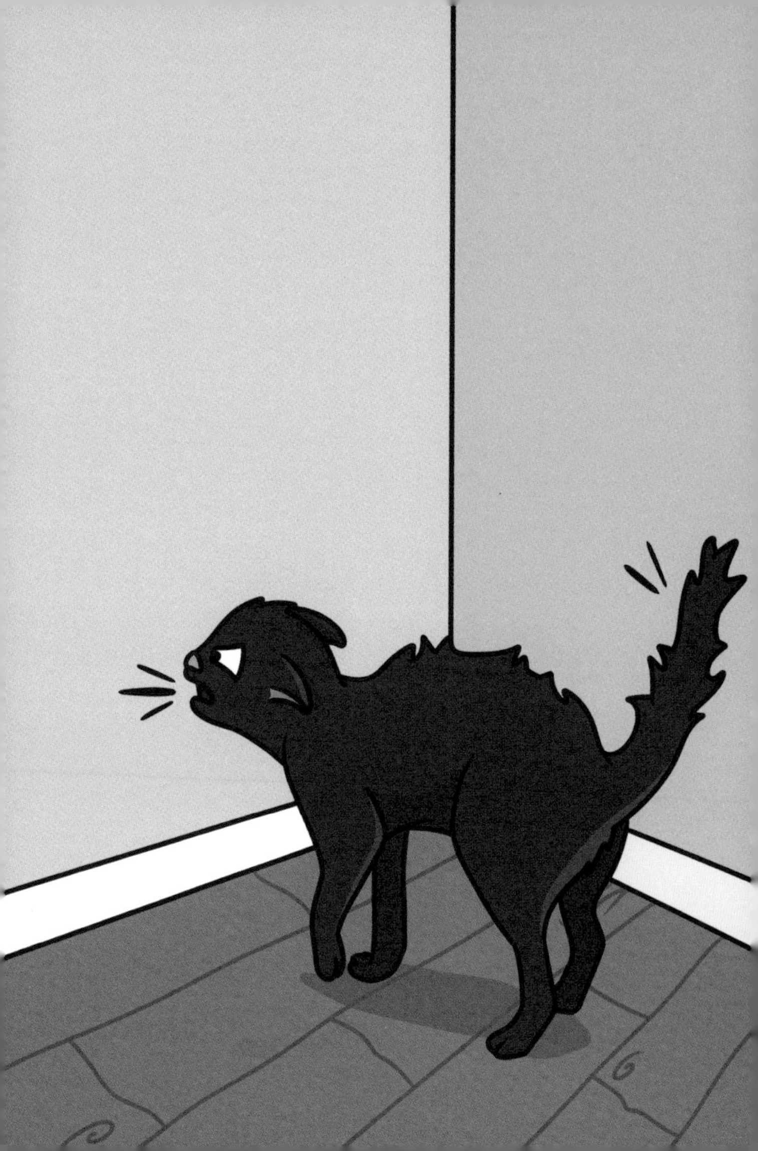

If your cat senses that one of your guests is nervous around felines, they will immediately do their best to put them at ease.

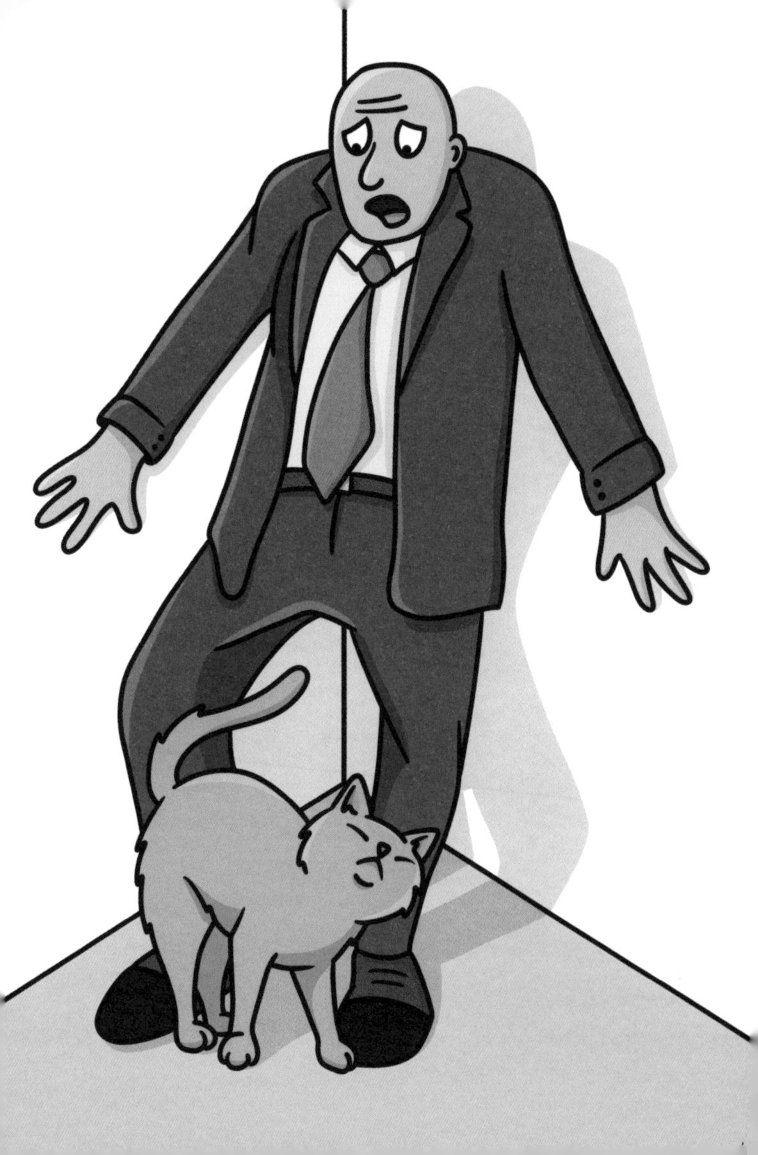

If you are planning
a board games night,
remember to provide
comfortable seating
for your cat.

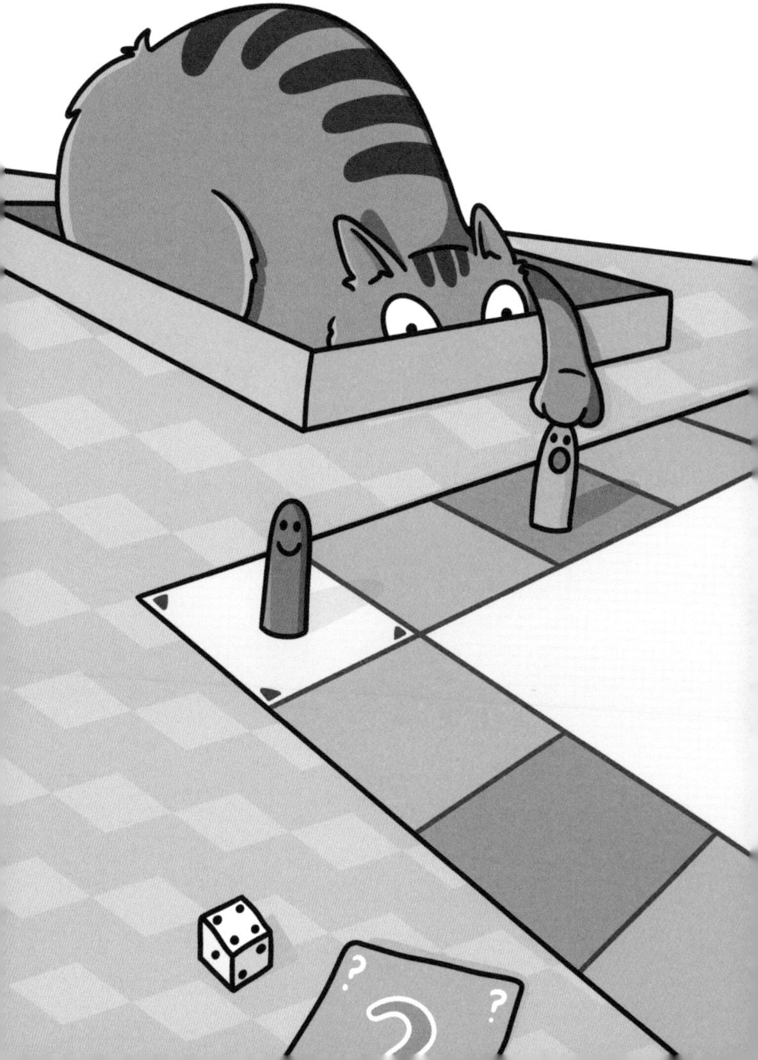

Know this:
your shoeless feet
are fair game.

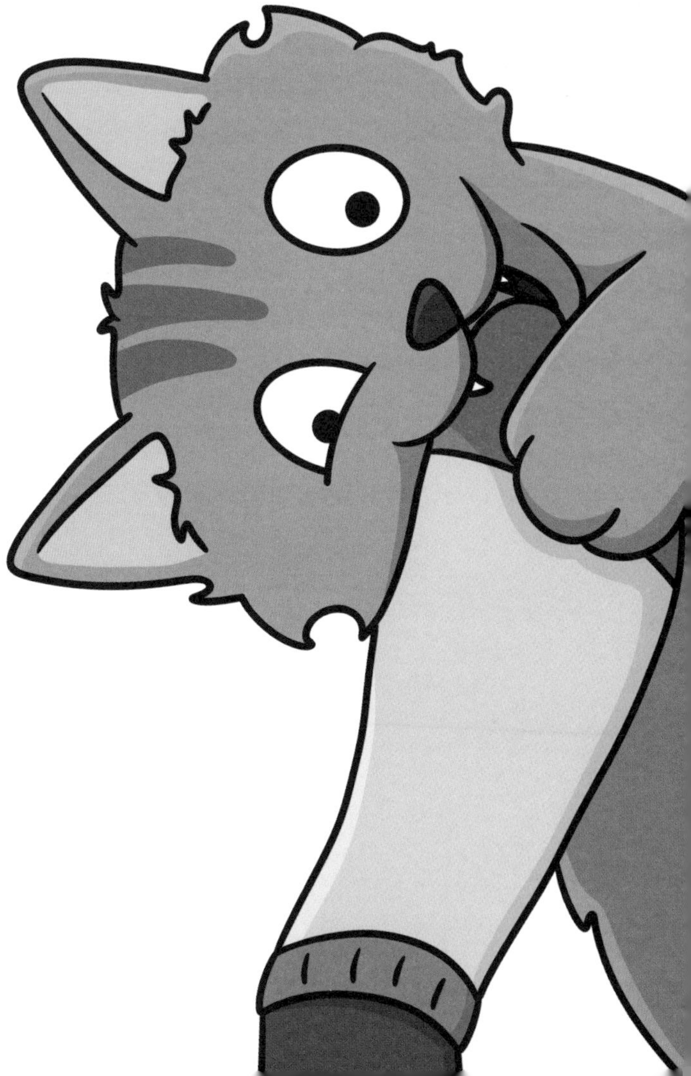

Trees are made
for climbing... up.
Be ready with a ladder
at any time, should your
feline require assistance
with their descent.

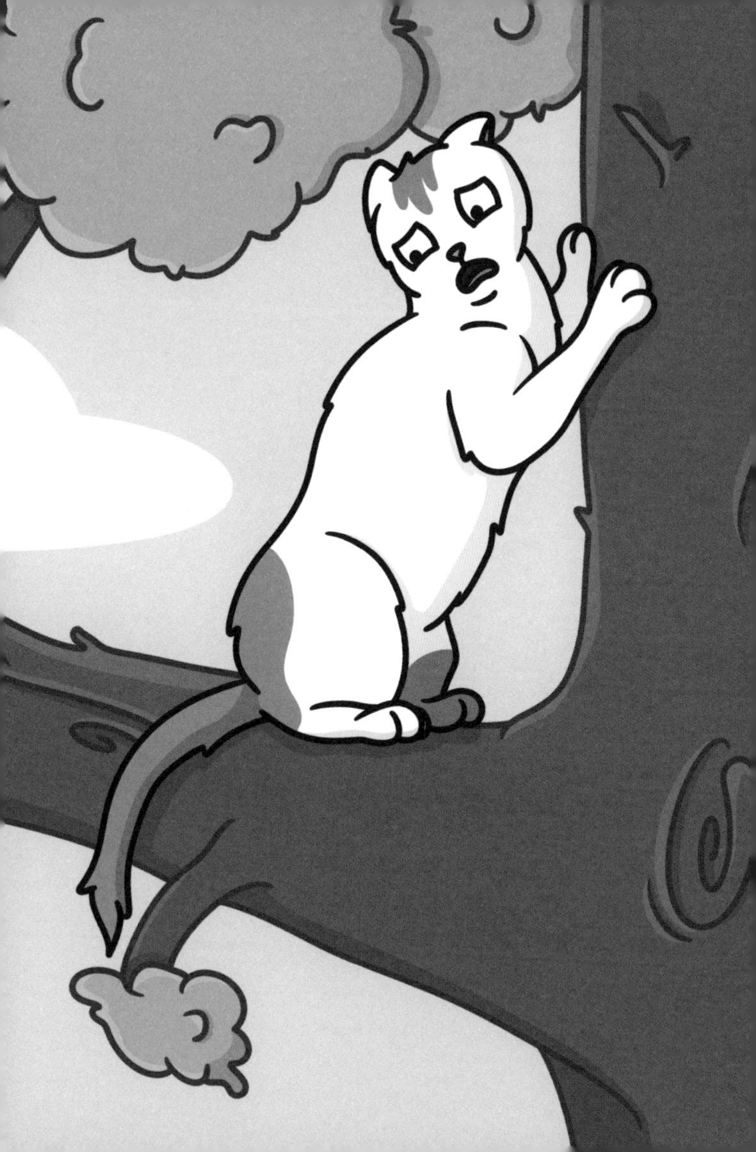

It is a truth universally acknowledged that a fresh toilet roll must be in want of unravelling.

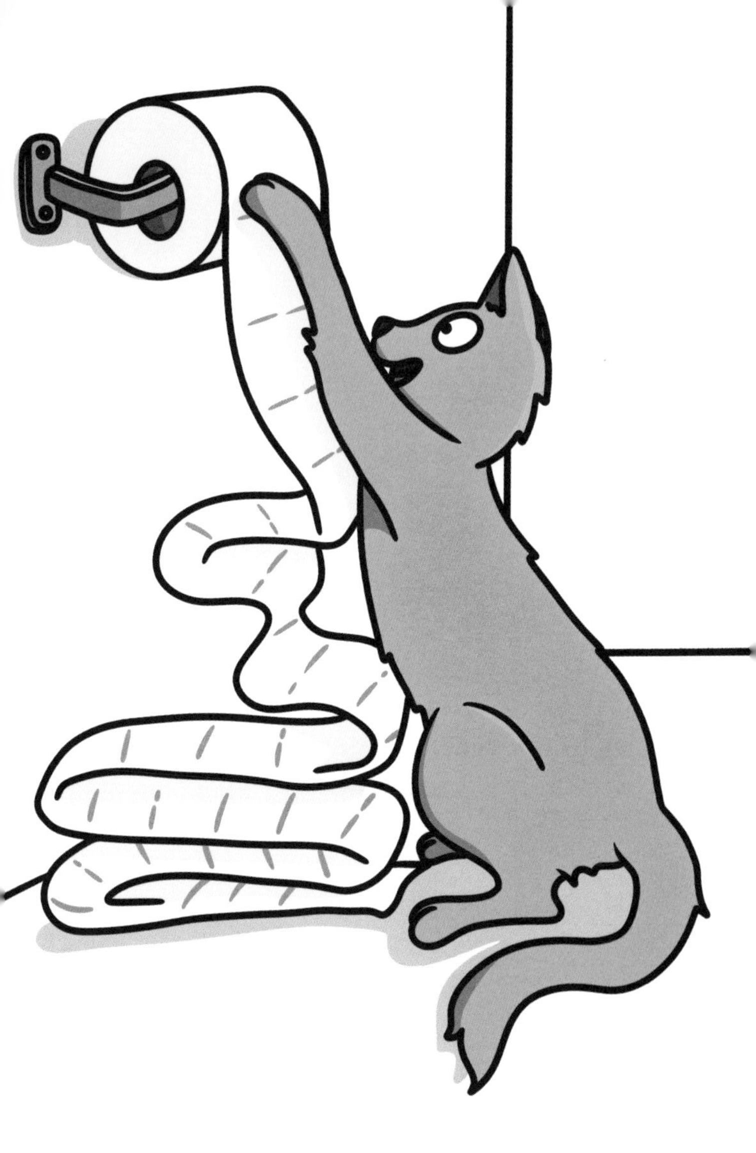

Closed doors are a
hazard and your cat will
alert you if they find
any around the home.

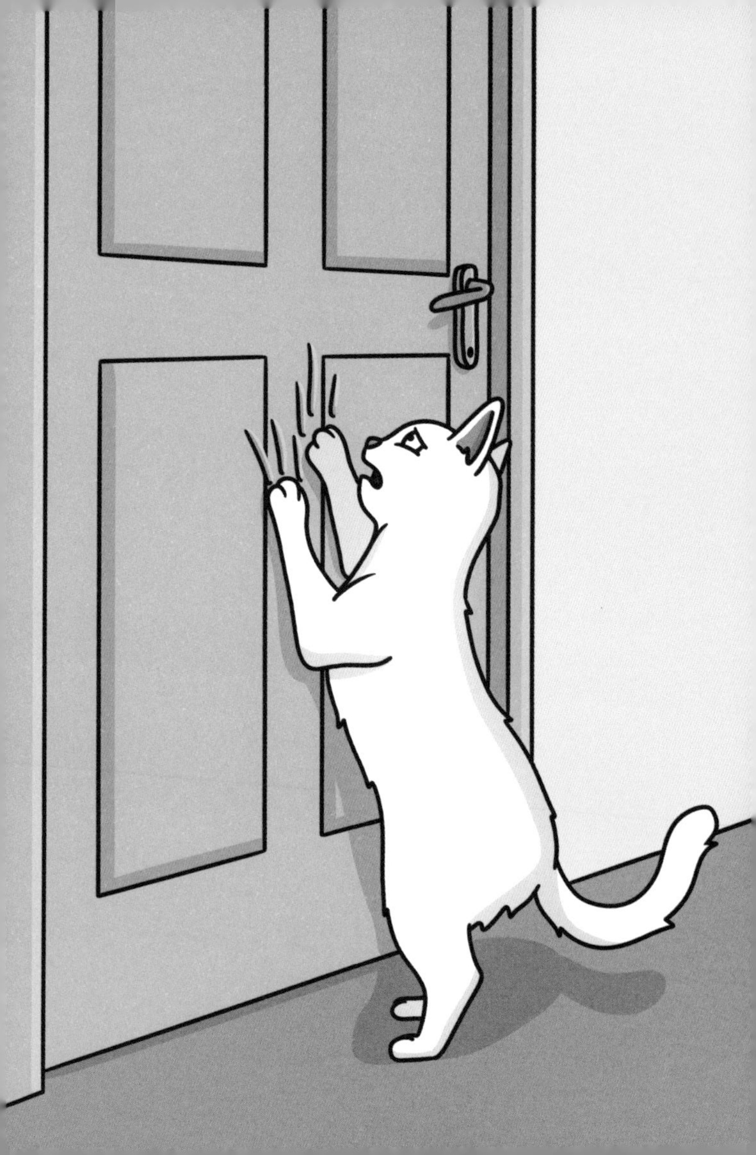

Cats are brilliant
linguists. You may be lucky
enough to observe yours
conversing with the local
bird population.

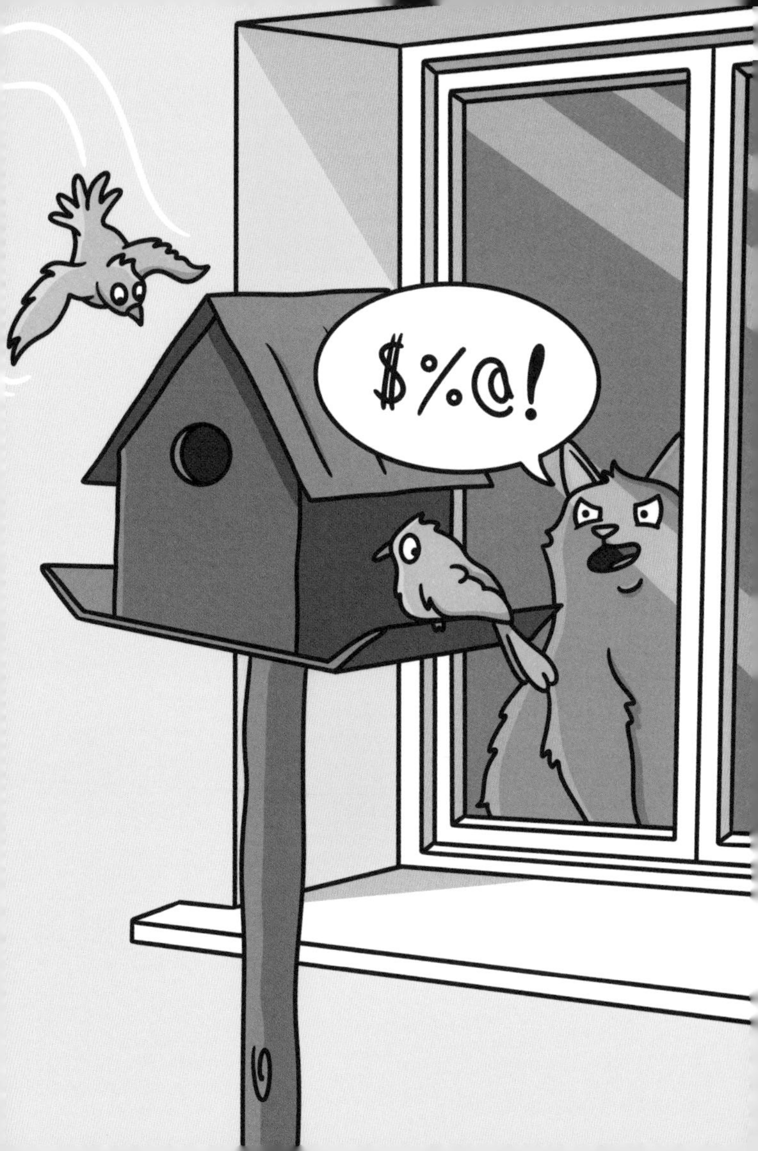
$%@!

Glass vases, fruit bowls
and empty boxes make
the perfect snuggle spots.
The smaller, the better!

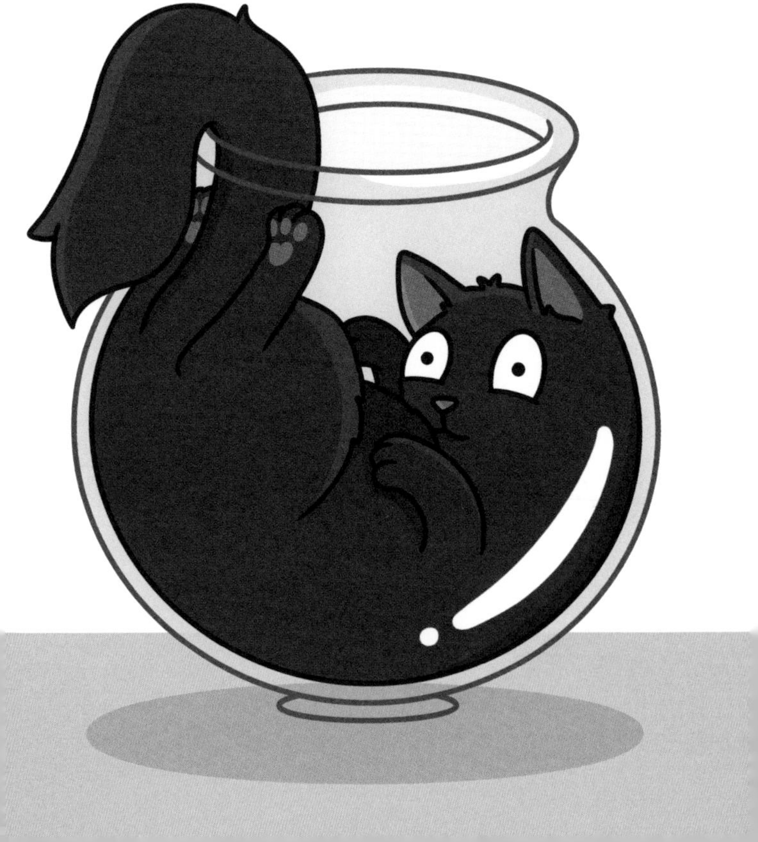

If you're wondering
where your missing socks
are, ask your cat.

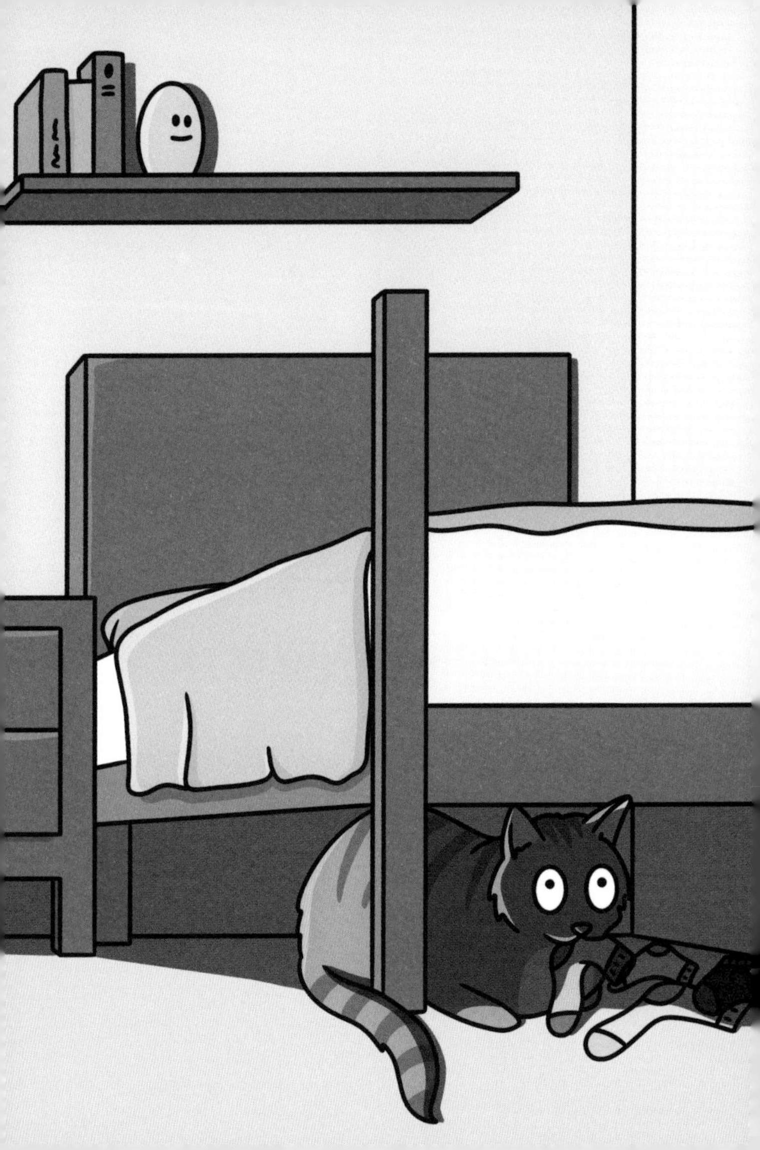

Above all, understand that
your cat is training you,
not the other way around.

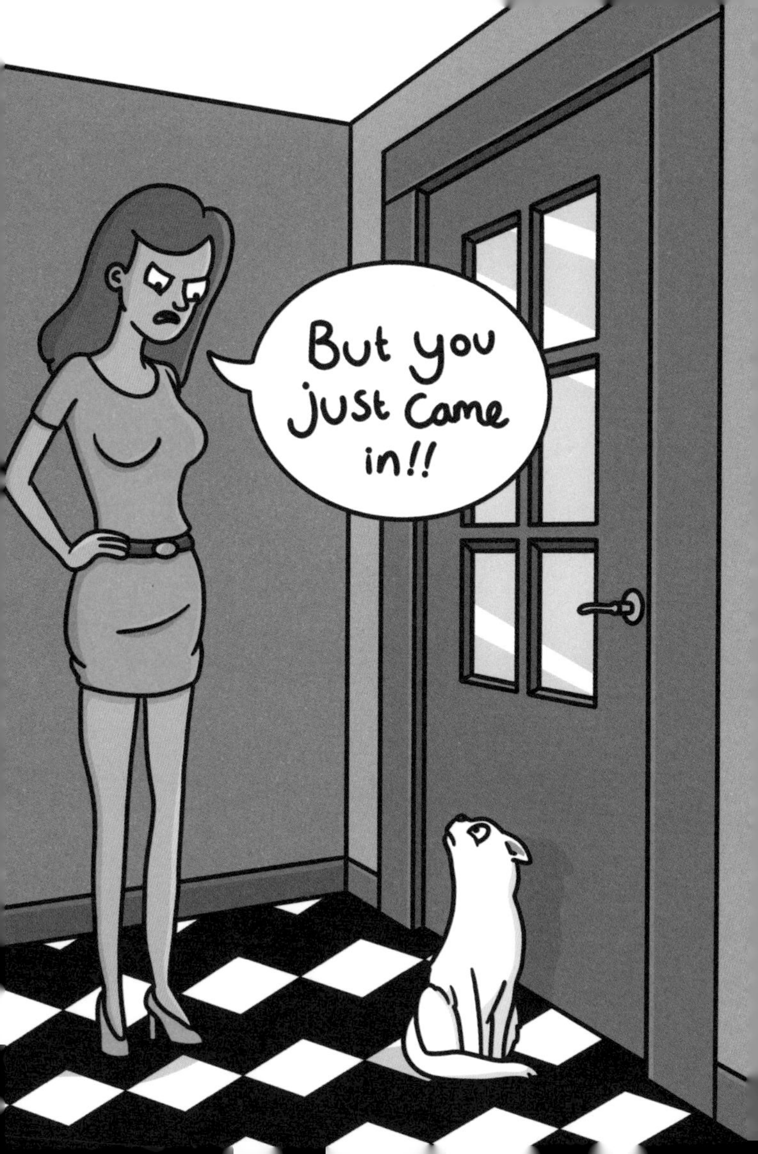
But you just came in!!

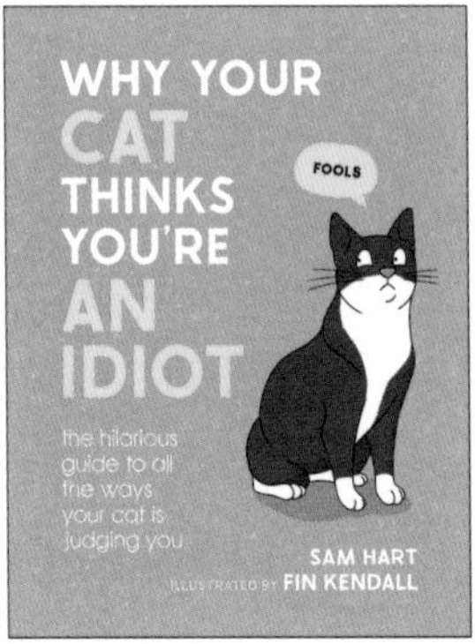
WHY YOUR CAT THINKS YOU'RE AN IDIOT
FOOLS
the hilarious guide to all the ways your cat is judging you
SAM HART
ILLUSTRATED BY FIN KENDALL

Why Your Cat Thinks You're An Idiot

Written by Sam Hart
Illustrated by Fin Kendall

978-1-80007-930-4

This frank and hilarious illustrated gift book is the perfect guide to why your cat thinks you are an idiot

From following you into the bathroom to knocking things off shelves, gain insight into the mind of your moggy and allow them to explain why they act the way they do.

Perfect for any cat lovers, or long-suffering owners, this book reveals the truth: your cat just thinks you are an idiot.

THE
CAT OWNER'S
SURVIVAL GUIDE
SOPHIE JOHNSON
ILLUSTRATED BY TATIANA DAVIDOVA

The Cat Owner's Survival Guide

Written by Sophie Johnson
Illustrated by Tatiana Davidova

978-1-80007-401-9

A hilarious, fully illustrated book full of tongue-in-cheek advice for surviving life as a cat parent – the perfect gift for any cat lover

This no-nonsense guide is here to teach you all the tricks you'll ever need to help you navigate life with your furry friend, so you can focus on the positives – like giving them head-scritches and cooing over their little toe beans.

Have you enjoyed this book?
If so, find us on Facebook
at Summersdale Publishers, on
Twitter/X at @Summersdale
and on Instagram and TikTok
at @summersdalebooks
and get in touch.
We'd love to hear from you!

www.summersdale.com